Do Pelicans Sip Nectar?

A Book About How Animals Eat

by Laura Purdie Salas

illustrated by Todd Ouren

PICTURE WINDOW BOOKS
Minneapolis, Minnesota

Special thanks to our advisers for their expertise:

Zoological Society of San Diego
San Diego Zoo, San Diego, California

Susan Kesselring, M.A., Literacy Educator
Rosemount–Apple Valley–Eagan (Minnesota) School District

Editor: Christianne Jones
Designer: Nathan Gassman
Page Production: Melissa Kes
Creative Director: Keith Griffin
Editorial Director: Carol Jones
The illustrations in this book were created digitally.

Picture Window Books
5115 Excelsior Boulevard
Suite 232
Minneapolis, MN 55416
877-845-8392
www.picturewindowbooks.com

Printed in the United States of America.

Library of Congress Cataloging-in-Publication Data
Salas, Laura Purdie.
Do pelicans sip nectar? : a book about how animals eat / by Laura Purdie Salas ; illustrated by
Todd Ouren.
p. cm. — (Animals all around)
Includes bibliographical references.
ISBN-13: 978-1-4048-2233-7 (hardcover)
ISBN-10: 1-4048-2233-X (hardcover)
1. Animals—Food—Juvenile literature. I. Ouren, Todd, ill. II. Title. III. Series.

QL756.5.S25 2007
591.5'3—dc22   2006003586

Editor's Note: There is often more than one species of each animal. The eating habits
described in this book are a general overview of each animal, unless a specific species is noted.

Do pelicans sip nectar?

No! Butterflies sip nectar.

A butterfly lands on a flower. It pokes its long, skinny proboscis inside the flower and slurps up sweet nectar. Flower pollen sticks to its feet. The butterfly tracks pollen from flower to flower. The pollen helps each flower grow new seeds.

Do pelicans have strainers
in their mouths?

No! Whales have strainers in their mouths.

Baleen whales have baleen plates instead of teeth. The plates let the water out but trap in tiny sea animals called zooplankton. The whales can then swallow their supper without all of the water.

Do pelicans hide their food?

No! Squirrels hide their food.

Squirrels gather and hide their food to survive the cold winter. They hide their food in different places. They might bury an acorn or hide it in a tree. If another animal finds some hidden food, the squirrels don't lose their entire winter supply.

Do pelicans trap their prey?

No! Spiders trap their prey.

Many spiders spin sticky silk webs. The web traps flies and other insects that land in it. Some spiders wrap the bugs in more silk. Then they hang them up by short threads and save them to eat later.

Do pelicans pick leaves
with their tongues?

No! Giraffes pick leaves with their tongues.

Giraffes wrap their long tongues around twigs and pull off the leaves. The giraffes' thick saliva coats any thorns that they may swallow. Giraffes can eat up to 75 pounds (34 kilograms) of food each day.

Do pelicans stretch their mouths wide open?

No! Snakes stretch their mouths wide open.

A snake can open its mouth incredibly wide. It can swallow food bigger than its own head. Stretchy tissues called ligaments connect a snake's upper and lower jaw. The two sides of the lower jaw can spread apart. A large python snake can even swallow an entire goat!

Do pelicans use rocks to get food?

No! Sea otters use rocks to get food.

Sea otters are one of the few animals that use tools to get food. They use small rocks to scrape shells off bigger rocks. Then they use a rock to smash open the shells so they can eat the animals inside. Sea otters especially like abalone, sea urchins, and clams.

Do pelicans sniff out dead food?

No! Vultures sniff out dead food.

Turkey vultures do not kill their food. Instead, they use their sense of smell and great eyesight to find dead animals. Vultures often eat other animals' leftovers. This helps keep wild areas clean.

Do pelicans tap trees
to find dinner?

No! Woodpeckers tap trees to find dinner.

Woodpeckers' favorite foods are termites and other small insects. These insects live underneath tree bark. Woodpeckers use their strong, sharp beaks to pound into the tree. This is how they uncover their food.

Do pelicans dive for their dinner?

Yes! Pelicans dive for their dinner.

A brown pelican dives into the water to catch fish. It uses its beak to scoop up 3 gallons (11 liters) of water and fish. Then the pelican drains out all of the water but keeps the fish. It tilts its beak toward the sky and swallows the fish in one big gulp.

Different Animal Eating Habits

Some animals have special body parts to help them find food.

•••••••••Woodpeckers have hard beaks to tap trees.

Whales strain water through their baleen to filter out the fish. •••••••••

••••Spiders spin webs from the silk their bodies make.

Snakes open their jaws wide to swallow large meals. ••••••••

••••Pelicans scoop up water and fish in their stretchy beak pouches.

Butterflies use their proboscis to drink nectar from flowers. •••••••••

•••••••••Giraffes use their long tongues to pick leaves.

Some animals use their sense of smell to find food.

Vultures sniff out dead animals. •••••••••••••••••••

Some animals use tools to find food.

•••••••••••Sea otters use rocks to smash open shells for food.

Some animals find hidden food.

Squirrels hide nuts and seeds for winter months. •••••••••••

Glossary

baleen—a bony plate that works like a strainer for trapping fish inside a whale's mouth

ligaments—tough, stretchy bands of tissue

nectar—sweet liquid inside a flower

pollen—a powder made by flowers to help them create new seeds

prey—an animal that is hunted by another animal for food

proboscis—a long, slender organ that looks like a straw

saliva—spit or juices in an animal's mouth

zooplankton—tiny animals in the ocean

To Learn More

At the Library

Altman, Joyce. *Lunch at the Zoo: What Zoo Animals Eat and Why.* New York: Henry Holt and Co., 2001.

Hickman, Pamela. *Animals Eating: How Animals Chomp, Chew, Slurp and Swallow.* Tonawanda, N.Y.: 2001.

Swanson, Diane. *Animals Eat the Weirdest Things.* New York: Holt, 1998.

On the Web

FactHound offers a safe, fun way to find Internet sites related to this book. All of the sites on FactHound have been researched by our staff.

1. Visit *www.facthound.com*
2. Type in this special code for age-appropriate sites: 140482233X
3. Click on the FETCH IT button.

Your trusty FactHound will fetch the best sites for you!

Index

butterflies, 4, 23
dive, 21, 22
giraffes, 12, 23
hide food, 7, 8, 23
pick leaves, 11, 12, 23
sea otters, 16, 23
sip nectar, 3, 4
snakes, 14, 23
sniff out food, 17, 18, 23
spiders, 10, 23

squirrels, 8, 23
strain water, 5, 6, 23
stretch ligaments, 13, 14
tap trees, 19, 20, 23
trap prey, 9, 10
use tools, 15, 16, 23
vultures, 18, 23
whales, 6, 23
woodpeckers, 20, 23

Look for all of the books in the Animals All Around series:

Do Bears Buzz? A Book About Animal Sounds
1-4048-0100-6

Do Bees Make Butter? A Book About Things Animals Make
1-4048-0288-6

Do Cows Eat Cake? A Book About What Animals Eat
1-4048-0101-4

Do Crocodiles Dance? A Book About Animal Habits
1-4048-2230-5

Do Dogs Make Dessert? A Book About How Animals Help Humans
1-4048-0289-4

Do Ducks Live in the Desert? A Book About Where Animals Live
1-4048-0290-8

Do Frogs Have Fur? A Book About Animal Coats and Coverings
1-4048-0292-4

Do Goldfish Gallop? A Book About Animal Movement
1-4048-0105-7

Do Lobsters Leap Waterfalls? A Book About Animal Migration
1-4048-2234-8

Do Parrots Have Pillows? A Book About Where Animals Sleep
1-4048-0104-9

Do Pelicans Sip Nectar? A Book About How Animals Eat
1-4048-2233-X

Do Penguins Have Puppies? A Book About Animal Babies
1-4048-0102-2

Do Polar Bears Snooze in Hollow trees? A Book About Animal Hibernation
1-4048-2231-3

Do Salamanders Spit? A Book About How Animals Protect Themselves
1-4048-0291-6

Do Squirrels Swarm? A Book About Animal Groups
1-4048-0287-8

Do Turtles Sleep in Treetops? A Book About Animal Homes
1-4048-2232-1

Do Whales Have Wings? A Book About Animal Bodies
1-4048-0103-0

Does an Elephant Fit in Your Hand? A Book About Animal Sizes
1-4048-2235-6